21st
Century
Skills Library

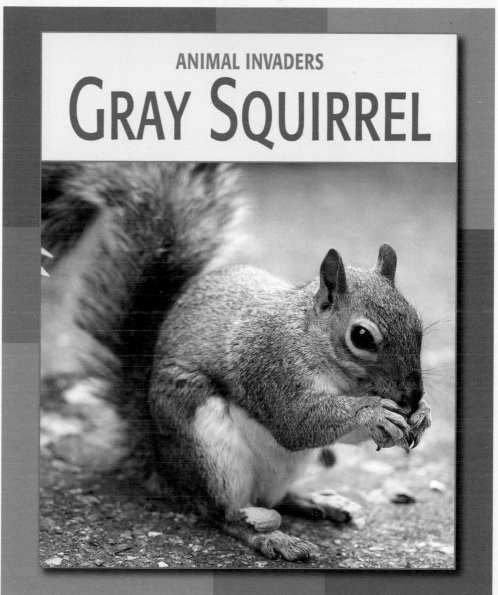

ANIMAL INVADERS
GRAY SQUIRREL

Barbara A. Somervill

Cherry Lake Publishing
Ann Arbor, Michigan

Published in the United States of America by Cherry Lake Publishing
Ann Arbor, MI
www.cherrylakepublishing.com

Content Adviser: Peter Lurz, PhD, University of Newcastle, Institute for Research on Environment and Sustainability, Newcastle upon Tyne, England

Please note: Our map is as up-to-date as possible at the time of publication.

Photo Credits: Cover and page 1, © iStockphoto.com/pjdodd; page 4, © USDA Forest Service-North Central Research Station Archive, USDA Forest Service, Bugwood.org; pages 7 and 25, © Joe Gough, used under license from Shutterstock, Inc.; page 8, © Michael Bishop, used under license from Shutterstock, Inc.; page 10, © iStockphoto. com/HelenMunro; page 12, © Photofrenetic/Alamy; page 14, © Christian Musat, used under license from Shutterstock, Inc.; page 17, © Terry Whittaker/Alamy; page 18, © iStockphoto.com/Westhoff; page 20, © Randy Cyr, GREENTREE Technologies, Bugwood.org; page 22, © Lisa F. Young, used under license from Shutterstock, Inc.

Map by XNR Productions Inc.

Library of Congress Cataloging-in-Publication Data
Somervill, Barbara A.
Gray squirrel / by Barbara A. Somervill.
 p. cm.—(Animal invaders)
Includes index.
ISBN-13: 978-1-60279-116-9
ISBN-10: 1-60279-116-3
1. Gray squirrel—Juvenile literature. I. Title. II. Series.
QL737.R68S646 2008
599.36'2—dc22   2007033511

*Cherry Lake Publishing would like to acknowledge the work of
The Partnership for 21st Century Skills.
Please visit www.21stcenturyskills.org for more information.*

TABLE OF CONTENTS

CHAPTER ONE

NOT ANOTHER GRAY SQUIRREL!

Gray squirrels can damage trees by stripping the bark away. Without its bark, a tree loses its protection.

In a valley outside Turin, Italy, a farmer looks at his grain field in dismay. Gray squirrels have been feeding on his maize crop. The damage is close to where the fields dip down to a stream.

For now, the squirrels have ruined less than 1 percent of the maize. The damage is not too bad. However, the farmer is concerned. He is worried that the damage to his crops will steadily increase.

To the northwest, in a forest in England, gray squirrels are taking over. They are doing what comes naturally to them—finding food. Gray squirrels are not native to England, but they like the area. The forests have plenty of food and few natural **predators**.

Unfortunately for the logging industry, squirrels sometimes feed by stripping bark from hardwood trees to get the softer wood and sap beneath. Various diseases and insects can attack trees without bark. And damaged trees produce stained and defective wood that can be hard to sell.

A **forester** examines a stand of trees marked for harvesting. Gray squirrels have left their mark. The

damage costs the British logging industry millions of U.S. dollars a year.

It is true that squirrels are not the only **mammals** damaging British woodlands. Deer, rabbits, and voles are also destructive. However, the nonnative gray squirrel continues to increase its range, competing with the native red squirrels for land.

People have brought the gray squirrel to Italy, England, and other places in Europe. Now different groups of people in those countries are facing the same question: what can they do to keep gray squirrels out of their forests, fields, and elsewhere?

CHAPTER TWO

More About Gray Squirrels

In a backyard in South Carolina, gray squirrels rush around burying acorns. The squirrels have buried them in the flower bed, stored some in holes in the gum trees, and hid others in firewood piled near the garage.

A gray squirrel holds an acorn in its paws.

South Carolina is one small part of the natural **habitat** for *Sciurus carolinensis*—the gray squirrel.

Squirrels are part of the natural cycle of life in the eastern United States and Canada. In their native habitat, squirrels eat insects, little birds, and small frogs. They also

*The underbelly of a gray squirrel is usually
lighter than the rest of its body.*

eat nuts and fruits, spreading seeds through their
normal range.

Eastern gray squirrels can be any shade of gray and even
black. Ears can be pale gray or even whitish in color. Males
and females have the same coloring.

Adult squirrels weigh from 12 to 24 ounces (340 to 680 grams). They measure about 16 to 20 inches (41 to 51 centimeters) long. The tail can measure nearly half the length of the body. Tails are useful for balance, communication with nearby squirrels, and protection from rain and the cold.

Males sometimes compete with each other for the chance to mate with females. Most squirrels mate after they are a year old. Squirrels usually breed in midwinter and again in late spring.

Most females produce two litters of young each year. Most litters have two to six kits. Newborns are hairless at birth and weigh barely 0.5 ounce (14 g). They

Much like a house cat, the gray squirrel uses whiskers on its face for touch.

have short whiskers called **vibrissae** that provide a sense of touch. Like humans, squirrels are mammals. Babies drink mother's milk. By 12 weeks, they are beginning to eat solid food.

Squirrels are hoarders. During the summer and fall, they collect and bury hundreds of acorns, nuts, and bulbs to eat during winter. Squirrels find their stored goodies by scent.

Although squirrels can build their own nests from twigs and leaves, they are happy to live in the crook of a tree. Or they may fight a woodpecker to take over its nesting site!

In their native range, squirrel populations do not expand out of control. Snakes, weasels, coyotes, red foxes, and raccoons prey on young and adult squirrels. Falcons, owls, hawks, and eagles swoop down and carry the squirrels away. Dogs and cats attack squirrels in backyards. In some areas, people hunt squirrels for food, and many squirrels are run over by cars on the streets. Outside of their native range, it's quite a different story.

Zoe Smolka is a red squirrel conservation officer in Scotland. She has seen how the advance of gray squirrels has affected red squirrel populations. She believes that people didn't understand the problems of bringing an alien animal onto their land. In a 2004 article in Scotland's *Sunday Herald*, Smolka spoke about the original introduction of gray squirrels. She said, "At the time, a lot of plants were being introduced to decorate gardens, and stately home owners seemed to think squirrels would make a nice addition. No one anticipated how successful they would be, or the serious consequences of their spread on the red squirrel population." Smolka is a member of the Red Squirrels in South Scotland Project, a conservation group working together to restore red squirrels to their native habitat.

CHAPTER THREE

GRAY INVADER

A gray squirrel rests on a public bench in London's Hyde Park.

Brought to England, Ireland, Italy, and South Africa for people's pleasure, eastern gray squirrels have quickly gone from pets to pests. People introduced gray squirrels in up to 33 places in England, Scotland, and Wales between 1876 and 1929. They released the animals straight into parks in Great Britain or tried to keep them as pets. But because squirrels do not make good pets, most were soon released into the wild.

In England, gray squirrels at the London Zoo were accidentally released, and they, too, spread out into local trees. The squirrels settled into their new home quickly and began producing kits.

Back in the United States, many predators keep the squirrel population under control. In England, however, most of those predators are not available. A pair of squirrels in England producing two litters of kits a year might end up with four or five kits surviving. Those kits become breeding adults quickly, and the gray squirrel population soon explodes out of control.

Despite disease, trapping, and shooting gray squirrels in England, the population spread throughout most of

The native red squirrel in Europe competes for survival with the invading gray squirrel from North America.

the country in about 50 years. Today, 2 million gray squirrels live in Great Britain, and that number is increasing all the time.

As gray squirrels thrive, the native red squirrels suffer. The populations of European red squirrel—*Sciurus vulgaris*—are declining at an alarming rate. Some conservationists think of gray squirrels as a "gray tide" sweeping through

England's forests. They believe gray squirrels are a major threat to the survival of the red squirrel.

Gray squirrels arrived in Ireland in 1911. The squirrels found the Irish countryside to be a fine habitat. The squirrels have since spread throughout eastern Ireland. They have even crossed the River Shannon!

It's the same in Italy, where people brought in gray squirrels as pets in the late 19th century. In 1948, two pairs were on the loose near Turin, Italy, and in 1966, five more gray squirrels were set free to roam a park near Genoa Nervi. In the beginning, the squirrels did not roam far from their release site. They soon increased their range looking for new food sources.

Italy poses more serious challenges than the islands of Great Britain and Ireland. Northern Italy connects to the rest of mainland Europe, specifically France and Switzerland. There are no water boundaries to contain the

squirrels within Italy. Current estimates are that gray squirrels will reach Switzerland within the next 20 years. Within the next 100 or 200 years, these critters are expected to spread throughout Europe and into western Asia.

Gray squirrels have also been introduced in the states of Texas and California as well as western Canada and South Africa. Perhaps because of the many natural predators in western North America and Africa, the squirrels seem to be less of a problem there than in Europe.

CHAPTER FOUR

PROBLEMS THEY CAUSE

This gray squirrel pokes its head into a wooden box protecting a bird nest in a British city garden.

Those cute, fuzzy gray critters that prance about the garden are major pests. They invade people's homes. They feed on farm crops. They destroy or damage trees, and they throw off the balance of nature where they do not belong.

When the weather is cold, and local trees are bare, a squirrel family can make a cozy home in an attic,

It can be difficult to trap a squirrel. This American red squirrel sits on top of a live trap—eating the bait without being captured!

basement, barn, or garage. They gnaw holes in the wood to get in and out. They burrow between the rafters and leave their waste there. Pest control agents set up traps to remove the creatures. But as many British homeowners have found, releasing the animals does not work. They always return.

Crop damage can be costly. In areas that grow grain, gray squirrels munch their way through corn, rye, wheat, oats, and barley. There is no safe, effective way to keep squirrels from crops.

But gray squirrels do the most damage to trees. They feed on the soft tree fiber and sap underneath the bark. Stripping bark all the way around the tree usually kills what's growing above this part of the tree. When stripping weakens the tree trunk, parts of the tree may snap off in the wind. Stripped trees can also suffer from slow growth, various infections, deformed trunks, staining, and rotting.

Because the squirrels destroy only some tree species, they affect the makeup

21st Century Content

Evaluating the costs of animal invaders is not an easy process. Scientists must study the species and see what damage it does to the economy, the environment, and the lives of people in the area. Some animal invaders damage crops, trees, homes, and buildings. Some invaders carry diseases or are poisonous. Do they affect livestock? Pets? Humans? All these factors, plus the cost of eliminating or controlling the species, add up to big money. In the United States alone, the cost of damage caused by animal and plant invaders as well as the cost of control programs have totaled billions of dollars in the last 50 years.

Squirrels have damaged this oak tree by gnawing around the hole where they nest.

of British forests. As the forest changes, its ability to support certain species also changes.

Europe's native squirrel, the red squirrel, is smaller than the gray squirrel and fares worse than the grays in the woodlands. While gray squirrels live comfortably in oak forests, red squirrels have had to adapt to life in **conifers** such as pines and spruces. They eat hazelnuts and seeds from conifer cones.

In the past 60 years, the red squirrel population has decreased dramatically. Reds and grays cannot live in the same area, although conservationists are not sure about all the reasons for the reds' decline. One problem is the squirrel pox carried by the grays. It can kill a red squirrel within two weeks. The grays are mostly resistant, however. They are also known to rob the reds' nut stores. They seem to adapt to habitats better than the red squirrels.

The gray squirrel population in England has reached 2.5 million, while the red squirrel population has sunk to fewer than 140,000. A program to save the red squirrel will be expensive. For the red squirrel survival plan to work, efforts to control the gray squirrel will need to be focused and effective.

Learning & Innovation Skills

Conservationists recognize that red squirrels need a mixed-conifer forest for survival. To help red squirrels, forest management is creating new homes for the red squirrels. Kielder Forest in England is now the United Kingdom's largest human-made forest. Kielder covers 148,265 acres (60,000 hectares) of land, of which 123,500 acres (50,000 ha) have been planted with mostly conifers. Sitka spruce covers 70 percent of the forest, along with Norway spruce, lodgepole pine, Scots pine, and larch. Red squirrels thrive in this environment. What do you think are the benefits to this kind of solution?

CHAPTER FIVE

POSSIBLE ANSWERS

Humans have caused the problem of gray squirrel invaders. It is up to them to solve it.

The answer for stopping the gray squirrel invasion in Europe is to remove these animals. The main challenge is also the source of the problem: humans. Humans brought the gray squirrels in; now they oppose many ways of bringing the squirrels under control.

In northwestern Italy, the National Wildlife Institute became concerned about the growing numbers of gray squirrels. Gray squirrels there were hurting red squirrel survival and damaging crops and woodlands.

In 1997, the institute came up with a plan to control the squirrels. Officials asked the Italian Health Ministry to stop allowing gray squirrels into Italy. The institute started trapping squirrels to test them for the squirrel pox and to kill them. They followed accepted **humane** methods.

The trapping program in Racconigi Park removed half the local squirrel population. A month later, animal-rights groups filed a lawsuit to stop the institute's plan. In court, the judge ruled against the institute for illegal hunting and cruelty to animals.

The lawsuit stopped the program, and the gray squirrel numbers in Italy are now soaring. Italy's red squirrel population is declining, and the lumber industry is

suffering. Gray squirrels are on the brink of moving beyond Italy and into Switzerland and France.

The situation in Italy is not unique. Plans to reduce gray squirrels in Scotland and England have met with some opposition, too.

Some conservationists have studied environments where gray squirrels do not run out of control. What prevents rapid expansion? The answers vary. It may be the number and success rate of squirrel predators. It may be the amount or quality of food. Or it could be natural boundaries such as rivers or high mountains or diseases that kill the squirrels. It may be a combination of things.

Are there natural solutions to controlling the gray squirrels in Europe? In the eastern United States, the larvae of an insect pest called the botfly might reduce squirrel populations.

When it comes to invasive species, there are no simple answers.

A skin disease called mange, caused by burrowing mites, also affects gray squirrels. As ways to control gray squirrels, though, these two **parasites** are not ideal. There is no way to control the parasites or limit their destruction to only gray squirrels.

One other possible natural solution might be increasing the numbers of meat-eating birds where gray squirrels are plentiful. More native owls, hawks, and gyrfalcons could help reduce squirrel populations. These species already live in Europe, so they would not be animal invaders. However, they would also prey on red squirrels, rabbits, hares, and mice.

Trapping, offering rewards for hunting the animals, and poisoning are common methods of removing squirrels. Where trapping is encouraged, wildlife management agencies recommend humane methods of killing the squirrels and burying the bodies. A reward system pays hunters for each squirrel pelt or tail brought to a conservation station. When poison bait is used, it is usually the effective, inexpensive poison called warfarin. But it can also poison pets, livestock, and native wildlife.

Finally, a sure cure for invasive species is to control breeding. In Great Britain, several research groups are studying the possibility of giving squirrels medicine to prevent them from producing young. Ongoing research is looking into ways to deliver this medicine to gray squirrels without affecting any other species.

By far, the best means of control is to prevent invasive species from coming into a country in the first place. The problems stemming from invasive species are many. The situation requires careful research and planning before taking any action. In the meantime, the squirrels continue to breed and expand. With any luck, it's not too late to stop the "gray tide" from rolling across Europe and into Asia.

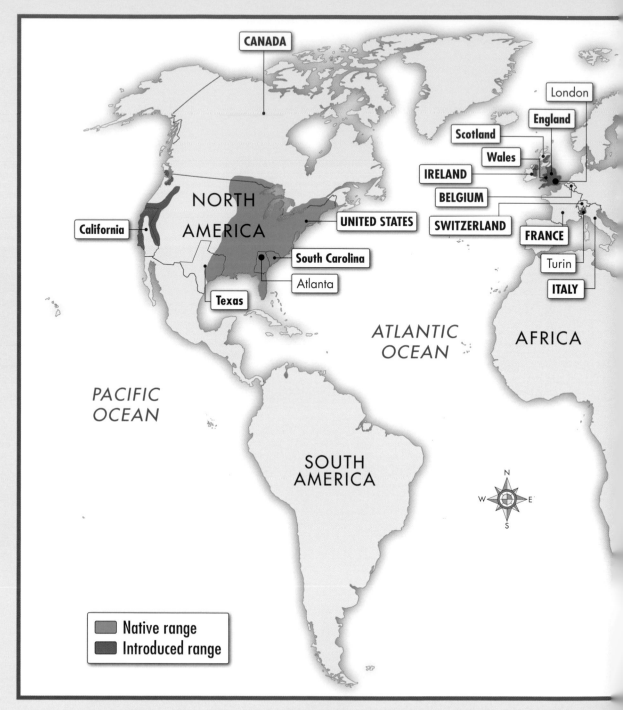

CANADA

London

England

Scotland

Wales

IRELAND

BELGIUM

SWITZERLAND

FRANCE

Turin

ITALY

NORTH AMERICA

California

UNITED STATES

South Carolina

Atlanta

Texas

ATLANTIC OCEAN

AFRICA

PACIFIC OCEAN

SOUTH AMERICA

N
W   E
S

Native range
Introduced range

This map shows where in the world the gray squirrel

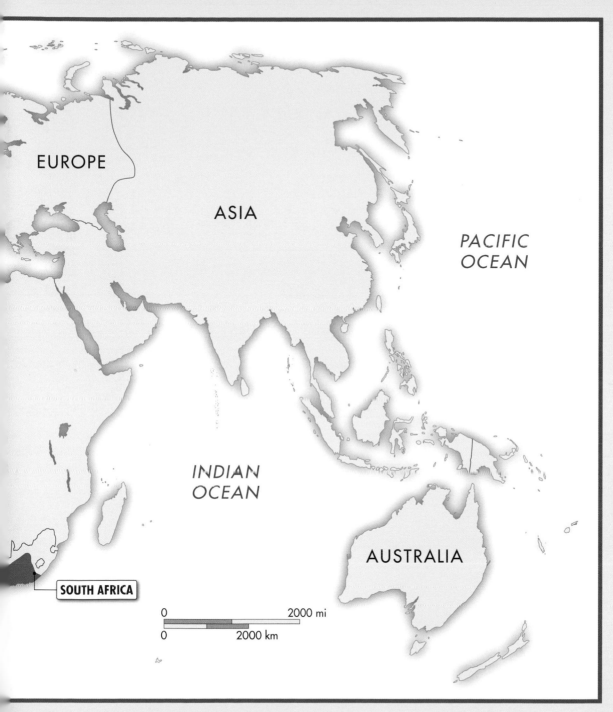

EUROPE

ASIA

PACIFIC OCEAN

INDIAN OCEAN

AUSTRALIA

SOUTH AFRICA

| 0 | 2000 mi |
| 0 | 2000 km |

lives naturally and where it has invaded.

GLOSSARY

conifers (KON-uh-furz) trees that produce cones; pine, fir, and spruce trees are conifers

conservation (kon-sur-VAY-shuhn) the preservation, management, and care of natural resources such as forests and wildlife

ecosystems (EE-koh-siss-tuhmz) communities of plants, animals, and other organisms together with their environment, working as a unit

forester (FOR-ist-uhr) a person trained in the science and work of developing and caring for forests

habitat (HAB-ih-tat) the area where a plant or an animal normally lives

humane (hyoo-MAYN) marked by not inflicting any more pain than necessary

mammals (MAM-uhlz) fur-bearing animals that bear live young

parasites (PEHR-uh-sites) plants or animals that grow, feed, and live in or on another animal or plant

predators (PRED-uh-turz) animals that hunt and eat other animals

species (SPEE-sheez) a group of similar plants or animals

vibrissae (vye-BRIH-see) the stiff, bristly whiskers of a mammal

zoonotic (zo-uh-NOH-tik) related to animal diseases that can be transmitted to humans; rabies is a zoonotic disease

For More Information

Books

Morgan, Sally. *Rodents*. North Mankato, MN: Chrysalis Education, 2004.

Murray, Peter. *Squirrels*. Chanhassen, MN: Child's World, 2006.

Somervill, Barbara A. *Forests*. Chanhassen, MN: Tradition Books, 2004.

Web Sites

BBC: Science and Nature Wildfacts
www.bbc.co.uk/nature/wildfacts/factfiles/190.shtml
To find out what is happening with gray squirrels in Great Britain

European Squirrel Initiative
www.europeansquirrelinitiative.org
For information about the gray squirrel's effect on the red squirrel in Great Britain

Hinterland Who's Who: Eastern Gray Squirrels
www.hww.ca/hww2.asp?id=89
To learn more about this backyard rodent

INDEX

ABOUT THE AUTHOR

Barbara A. Somervill writes children's nonfiction books on a variety of topics. She is particularly interested in nature and foreign countries. Somervill believes that researching new and different topics makes writing every book an adventure. When she is not writing, Somervill is an avid reader and plays bridge.